Language Expansion for Autism
Third Edition

Terresa York, MNM

Original artwork: Chad Jones
Graphic design: Jason Moore

Printed in the United States of America

10 9 8 7 6 5 4

First Edition Printing 2006, ©2006, Terresa York ISBN 978-1-4303-0577-4
Second Edition Printing 2010, ©2009, Terresa York ISBN 978-0-9826035-0-5
Third Edition Printing 2016, ©2016, Terresa York ISBN 978-0-9826035-2-9

ALL RIGHTS RESERVED

No part of this publication may be reproduced, stored, distributed, or introduced into a retrieval system, or transmitted, in any form, or by any means (electronic, mechanical, digital, photocopy, or otherwise), without permission of both the copyright owner and the publisher.

Electronic piracy of copyrighted materials is against the law: The scanning, uploading, and/or distribution of this book via the Internet or via any other means without the permission of the publisher are illegal and punishable by law.

If you purchased this book without a cover, you should be aware that this book is stolen property. It was reported as "unsold and destroyed" to the publisher, and neither the author nor the publisher has received any payment for this "stripped book."

©2016 Terresa York (third edition)

NAKIA◆E

ISBN 978-0-9826035-2-9

http://www.nashobasworkbooks.com

PREFACE

Prerequisite Skills

As a prerequisite, it is assumed that the child has basic reading skills and can write simple answers when prompted.

How to use Nashoba's "WH" Workbook

This workbook is designed to gradually increase a child's ability to answer "wh" questions through practice and repetition utilizing simple, visual, concrete formats. Color cues and prompts are used throughout the book to assist the child in formulating questions and answers and are gradually faded out as the lessons progress.

The goal is not to complete the work but to learn the skill. Lessons can and should be repeated as many times as necessary; pictures or examples from home, school, magazines and books can be used to expand the lessons and provide increased practice and repetition. The suggested activities listed at the end are intended to help the child generalize the emerging skills into other settings.

Other Helpful Hints

While each child should have their own book in order to keep notes, personal progress, and data portable in one format, you may want to photo copy lessons as you go along in case the child has trouble with any particular lesson. In that case, it would be good to repeat the lesson as many times as necessary before moving on.

CONTENTS

PART ONE: Why – Because .... page 8

PART TWO: When .... page 14

PART THREE: Where .... page 20

PART FOUR: Who .... page 22

PART FIVE: What .... page 24

PART SIX: What verses Who .... page 25

PART SEVEN: Who, What, or Where .... page 32

PART EIGHT: Who, What, and How .... page 35

PART NINE: Who, What, Where, & Why Stories .... page 37

PART TEN: Who, When, and Why .... page 43

PART ELEVEN: Reasoning Why .... page 47

PART TWELVE: Putting it All Together .... page 52

SUGGESTED FOLLOW UP ACTIVITIES .... page 64

DATA COLLECTION & NOTES .... page 65

OTHER AVAILABLE WORKBOOKS AND MATERIALS .... page 74

PART ONE
WHY – BECAUSE

The Why – Because section explores the reason why things occur. Read the simple sentences and answer the "why" questions. Don't forget to use end punctuation.

Joseph cried because he skinned his knee.

Why did Joseph cry? Because _____

Sally smiled because she ate some candy.

Why did Sally smile? Because _____

Joe laughed because his dad tickled him.

Why did Joe laugh? Because _____

Tony ran because the dog chased him.

Why did Tony run? Because _____

Shannon screamed because Lisa scared her.

Why did Shannon scream? Because _____

Mom got mad because dad spilled his drink.

Why did mom get mad? _____

Sarah called because Sue asked her to.

Why did Sarah call? _____

Mary ate an apple because she was hungry.

Why did Mary eat an apple? Because _____

Tom came inside because it was time for dinner.

Why did Tom come inside? Because _____

Joe ran because his sister chased him.

Why did Joe run? Because _____

Mike brushed his teeth because it was bed time.

Why did Mike brush his teeth? Because _____

Ellen ate her ice cream because she liked it.

Why did Ellen eat her ice cream? Because _____

Sue was sad because she lost her toy.

Why was Sue sad? _____

The dog barked because the doorbell rang.

Why did the dog bark? _____

Lucy took a nap because her dad told her to.

Why did Lucy take a nap? _____

Andy put on his hat because it was cold outside.

Why did Andy put on his hat? _____

The word "because" does not always appear in a sentence, but we can still reason why something occurred. Answer the "why" questions below. Don't forget your punctuation.

Example

Sally brought her baseball glove to the baseball game.

Why did Sally bring her baseball glove?

(Any of the below answers would be correct.)

Because she was going to a baseball game.

Because she planned on playing baseball.

Because she needed a glove to play baseball.

Because she wanted to play baseball.

Sharon bought a present for Lee's birthday party?

Why did Sharon buy a present?

Because _____

Jacob used his money to buy some candy?

Why did Jacob use his money?

Because _____

Michael brought his basketball to the basketball game.

Why did Michael bring his basketball to the game?

Because _____

Steven took his pencil to school.

Why did Steven take his pencil to school?

Because _____

Larry put on his pajamas before bed.

Why did Larry put on his pajamas?

Because _____

Kate made popcorn before the movie.

Why did Kate make popcorn?

Because _____

Cindy put a leash on her dog before walking him.

Why did Cindy put a leash on her dog?

Because _____

Sarah turned off the light before she got in bed.

Why did Sarah turn off the light?

Because _____

Michael brought his baseball bat to the baseball game.

Why did Michael bring his baseball bat to the game?

Because _____

Steven took his lunch to school.

Why did Steven take his lunch to school?

Because _____

Larry said goodnight to his sister before he went to bed.

Why did Larry say goodnight to his sister?

Because _____

Kate made a Christmas card for her mom?

Why did Kate make a Christmas card?

Because _____

Cindy gave her dirty dog a bath.

Why did Cindy give her dog a bath?

Because _____

Sarah called Lulu on the telephone to say hello.

Why did Sarah call Lulu?

Because _____

John washed his apple before he ate it.

Why did John wash his apple?

Because _____

Lisa peeled her banana before she ate it.

Why did Lisa peel her banana?

Because _____

Kari counted her money before she went to the store.

Why did Kari count her money?

Because _____

PART TWO
WHEN

The word "when" refers to the time something happened. This may be an actual time like *four o'clock*, or it could be a more general time like *first thing in the morning*. Answer the "when" questions.

Example

Pete will get a gold star after he finishes his math.

When will Pete get a gold star? After he finishes his math.

Joe will play with Ted after dinner.

When will Joe play with Ted? _____

Mom will pick up Lou at two o'clock.

When will mom pick up Lou? _____

Tina will call Theresa after school.

When will Tina call Theresa? _____

Harry will brush his teeth before bed.

When will Harry brush his teeth? _____

Jim will eat his chips during lunch.

When will Jim eat his chips? _____

Tony will go to the zoo on Saturday.

When will Tony go to the zoo? _____

Mom will wash our clothes when they get dirty.

When will Mom wash our clothes? _____

We will play all day when we get to grandma's house.

When will we play all day? _____

The dog will take off running when he gets to the park.

When will the dog take off running? _____

The cat will purr when Rachel pets her.

When will the cat purr? _____

The moon will come out when the sun goes down.

When will the moon come out? _____

Now YOU write the "when" questions!

Don't forget the question mark at the end of your sentence.

<mark>Example</mark>

The teacher will *reward her student* when he is done working.

When will **the teacher reward her student?**

Answer: when he is done working.

The dog will whimper when I pull his tail.

When will _____

Answer: when I pull his tail.

The cat will run away when she gets wet.

When _____

Answer: when she gets wet.

The leaves will fall off the trees in autumn.

When _____

Answer: in autumn.

The snow will fall in the winter.

When _____

Answer: in the winter.

The sun will rise in the morning.

When _____

Answer: in the morning.

The moon will come out at night.

_____

Answer: at night.

The rainbow will appear after the rain stops.

_____

Answer: after the rain stops.

The sun will come out tomorrow.

_____

Answer: tomorrow.

The movie will be released in August.

_____

Answer: in August.

This time, you write the "when" questions AND the answers!

Don't forget your end punctuation.

Example

The snow will melt when the sun comes out.

Question: **When will the snow melt?**

Answer: **When the sun comes out.**

The dog will bark when the mailman comes to the door.

Question: _____

Answer: _____

The train will pull into the station at seven o'clock.

Question: _____

Answer: _____

The truck driver will stop driving when he gets tired.

Question: _____

Answer: _____

The dancer will bow when she is done dancing.

Question: _____

Answer: _____

The flowers will bloom in the spring.

Question: _____

Answer: _____

The phone will ring when Johnny calls.

Question: _____

Answer: _____

The curtain will close when the play is over.

Question: _____

Answer: _____

The bell will ring at the start of each hour.

Question: _____

Answer: _____

The singer will perform at half-time.

Question: _____

Answer: _____

PART THREE
WHERE

The word "where" refers to a place. Answer the "where" questions.

Example

Mom will take me to school in the morning.

Where will mom take me in the morning? **To school**

Joe will play with Ted at the park.

Where will Joe play with Ted? _____

Dad will take me to the store to buy a toy.

Where will dad take me to buy a toy? _____

Grandma will give me a kiss on the nose when I laugh.

Where will grandma kiss me when I laugh? _____

Grandpa will take me to the baseball game to watch my favorite teams.

Where will grandpa take me to watch my favorite teams?

_____

The kids went to play in the cabin.

Where did the kids go to play? _____

John went to the park to ride his skateboard.

Where did John go to ride his skateboard? _____

Dad went to the ballpark to see his favorite team.

Where did dad go to see his favorite team? _____

Amanda went to the grocery store to buy a pear.

Where did Amanda go to buy a pear? _____

Lilly went to the pet store to buy a fish.

Where did Lilly go to buy a fish? _____

Aaron went to the sports store to buy a basketball.

Where did Aaron go to buy a basketball? _____

The girl went to the mountains to see the snow.

Where did the girl go to see the snow? _____

PART FOUR
WHO

The word "who" refers to a person. Answer the "who" questions.

Example

Mom will take me to school in the morning.

Who will take me to school in the morning? Mom

Dad will take me to the store to buy a toy.

Who will take me to the store to buy a toy? _____

Grandma will give me a kiss on the nose when I laugh.

Who will give me a kiss when I laugh? _____

Grandpa will take me to the baseball game to watch my favorite teams.

Who will take me to watch my favorite teams? _____

The kids went to play in the cabin.

Who went to play in the cabin? _____

John went to the park to ride his skateboard.

Who went to the park to ride his skateboard? _____

Dad went to the ballpark to see his favorite team.

Who went to the park to see his favorite team? _____

Amanda went to the grocery store to buy a pear.

Who went to the grocery store to buy a pear? _____

Lilly went to the pet store to buy a fish.

Who went to the pet store to buy a fish? _____

Aaron went to the sports store to buy a basketball.

Who went to the sports store to buy a basketball? _____

The girl went to the mountains to see the snow.

Who went to the mountains to see the snow? _____

The teacher told the children to sit quietly.

Who told the children to sit quietly? _____

The clown bowed after his circus act.

Who bowed after his circus act? _____

PART FIVE
WHAT

"What" refers to a thing (an object) or an animal. Answer the "what" questions below.

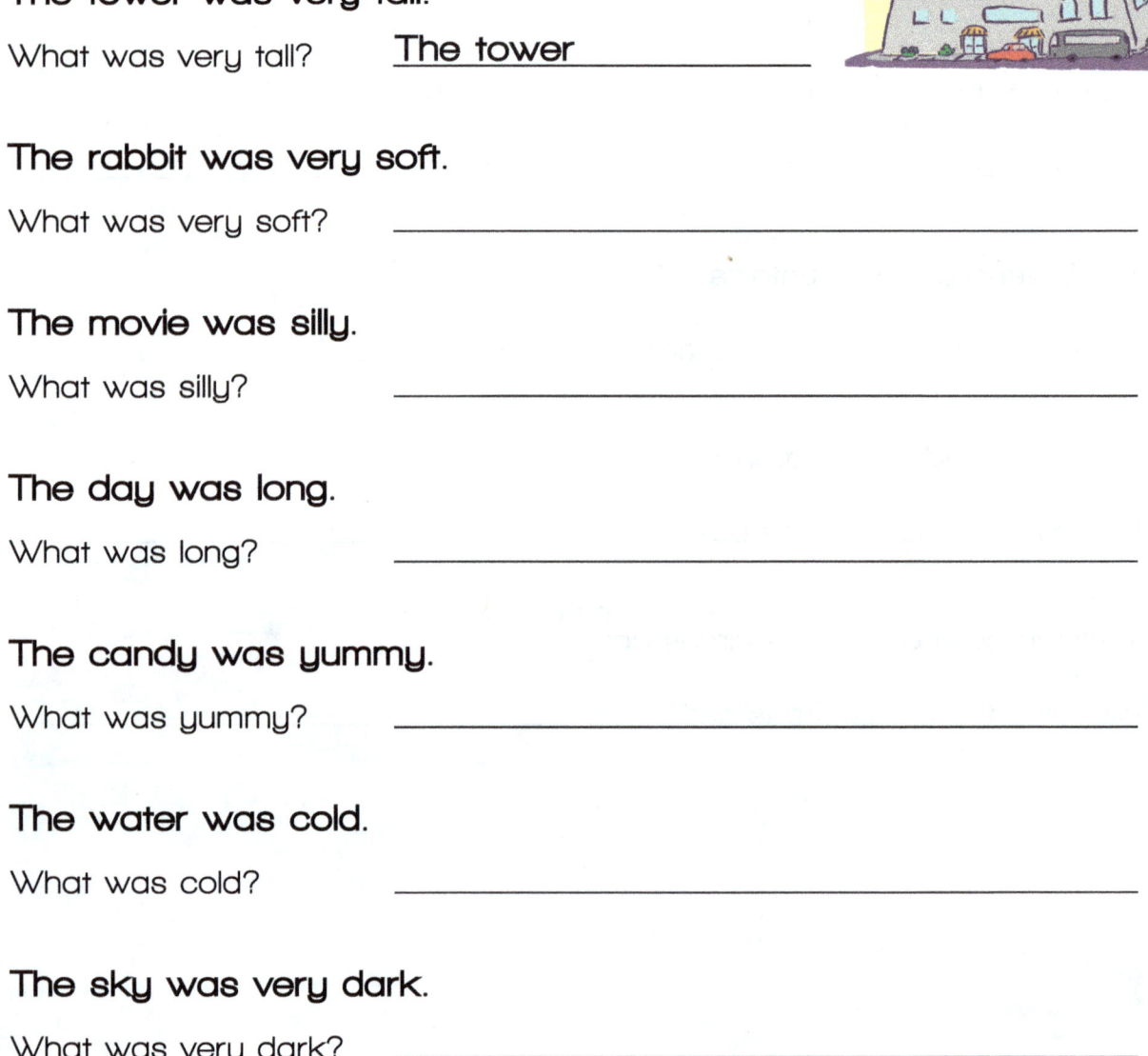

Example

The tower was very tall.

What was very tall?   The tower

The rabbit was very soft.

What was very soft?   _____

The movie was silly.

What was silly?   _____

The day was long.

What was long?   _____

The candy was yummy.

What was yummy?   _____

The water was cold.

What was cold?   _____

The sky was very dark.

What was very dark?   _____

PART SIX
WHAT VERSES WHO

1. We already know that "who" refers to a person, and that sometimes a person has a name.

   WHO = A PERSON

   Example

The lady had brown hair.	Who had brown hair?	The lady.
Ms. Parker had brown hair.	Who had brown hair?	Ms. Parker.

2. We also learned that "what" refers to a thing or an animal.

   WHAT = THING OR ANIMAL

   Example

The lake was deep.	What was deep?	The lake.
The car was red.	What was red?	The car.
The goat was white.	What was white?	The goat.
The dog was little.	What was little?	The dog.

3. But what happens when an animal is given a name? Then we refer to the animal, only if it has a name, as a "who".

   WHO = PERSON OR A NAME

   Example

The goat was white.	What was white?	The goat.
Mike the goat was white.	Who was white?	Mike the goat.
Mike was white.	Who was white?	Mike.
The dog was little.	What was little?	The dog.
Rex the dog was little.	Who was little?	Rex the dog.
Rex was little.	Who was little?	Rex.

Let's practice WHAT verses WHO. Fill in the blanks.

What = Thing or Animal   Who = Person or Name

Dog	=	Animal	=	What
Cat	=	_____	=	_____
Cow	=	_____	=	_____
Man	=	Person	=	_____
Woman	=	_____	=	_____
Girl	=	_____	=	_____
Car	=	Thing	=	_____
Boat	=	_____	=	_____
Ship	=	_____	=	_____
Alvin the Dog	=	Name	=	_____
Fluffy the Cat	=	_____	=	_____
Betsy the Cow	=	_____	=	_____

What = Thing or Animal			Who = Person or Name
Frog	= Animal	=	What
Mr. Johnson	= _____	=	_____
Mrs. Johnson	= _____	=	_____
Sarah Johnson	= _____	=	_____
Plant	= _____	=	_____
Tree	= _____	=	_____
Rock	= _____	=	_____
Airplane	= _____	=	_____
Susie the worm	= _____	=	_____
Mary the butterfly	= _____	=	_____
Tony the Tiger	= _____	=	_____
Johnny	= _____	=	_____
Frank	= _____	=	_____

Louis	=	_____	=	_____
The Dentist	=	_____	=	_____
The Doctor	=	_____	=	_____
Television	=	_____	=	_____
Wind	=	_____	=	_____
Lamp	=	_____	=	_____
Spider	=	_____	=	_____
Charlotte the Spider	=	_____	=	_____
Horse	=	_____	=	_____
Joe the Horse	=	_____	=	_____
Frog	=	_____	=	_____
Kermit the Frog	=	_____	=	_____
Chair	=	_____	=	_____
Watch	=	_____	=	_____

Now let's practice asking questions:

> What = Thing or Animal   Who = Person or Name

Example

The dog was fat.

A dog is a (circle) → Person   Name   (Animal)   Thing

Who   (What) → __What_____ was fat?

The boy was cute.

A boy is a (circle) → Person   Name   Animal   Thing

Who   What → _____ was cute?

The elephant has long tusks.

An elephant is an (circle)   Person   Name   Animal   Thing

Who   What   _____ has long tusks?

Dumbo the elephant has long tusks.

Dumbo the elephant is a (circle)   Person   Name   Animal   Thing

Who   What   _____ has long tusks?

The truck was red.

A truck is a (circle)   Person   Name   Animal   Thing

Who   What   _____ was red?

The chair was hard.

A chair is a (circle)   Person   Name   Animal   Thing

Who   What   _____ was hard?

The watch was old.

A watch is a (circle)　　　　　　　Person　　　Name　　　Animal　　　Thing

Who　　(What)　　　　　　　　　**What**_____ was old?

Susan was cute.

Susan is a (circle)　　　　　　　　Person　　　Name　　　Animal　　　Thing

Who　　What　　　　　　　　　_____ was cute?

The stereo has big speakers.

A stereo is a (circle)　　　　　　　Person　　　Name　　　Animal　　　Thing

Who　　What　　　　　　　　　_____ has big speakers?

Jay the flying dragon was green.

Jay the flying dragon is a (circle)　Person　　　Name　　　Animal　　　Thing

Who　　What　　　　　　　　　_____ is green?

The couch was soft.

A couch is a (circle)　　　　　　　Person　　　Name　　　Animal　　　Thing

Who　　What　　　　　　　　　_____ was soft?

The cow was spotted.

A cow is an (circle)　　　　　　　Person　　　Name　　　Animal　　　Thing

Who　　What　　　　　　　　　_____ was spotted?

The concert was long.

A concert is a (circle)　　　　　　Person　　　Name　　　Animal　　　Thing

Who　　What　　　　　　　　　_____ was long?

What or Who?

Circle "what" or "who" then write and answer the questions.

What = Things or Animals.   Who = People or Names.

Example

The rabbit was very furry.   Circle One: (What?)   Who?

__What__ was very furry?   The rabbit

The boy was silly.   Circle One: What?   __Who?__

_____ was silly?   _____

The woman had long hair.   Circle One: What?   Who?

_____ had long hair?   _____

The man was laughing.   Circle One: What?   Who?

_____ was laughing?   _____

The clown was cold..   Circle One: What?   Who?

_____ was cold?   _____

The sky was very dark.   Circle One: What?   Who?

_____ was very dark?   _____

The night was long.   Circle One: What?   Who?

_____ was long?   _____

PART SEVEN
WHO, WHAT, OR WHERE?

Write "who, what, or where" to begin the question and fill in the answer. Don't forget your punctuation and to capitalize names.

Who = People   What = Things or Animals   Where = Place

Sentence	Who? What? Where? Question	Answer
Example		
Stacy went to Alaska.	Who went to Alaska?	Stacy
Jill went to Ohio.	_____ did Jill go?	To Ohio
Stacy had fun.	_____ did Stacy do?	Have fun
Sharon flew to Rome.	_____ went to Rome?	_____
Tracy flew to Spain.	_____ went to Spain?	_____
Sharon wrote home.	_____ did Sharon do?	_____
Mary ate an apple.	_____ did Mary eat?	_____
Tom ate a banana.	_____?	_____
Mary threw away the core.	_____ did Mary do?	_____
John went home.	_____ did John go?	_____
Joe threw a ball.	_____ did Joe do?	_____
Mike went to school.	_____ went to school?	_____
John went home.	_____ did John go?	_____
Joe threw a ball.	_____ did Joe do?	_____
Mike went to school.	_____ went to school?	_____

Who = People	What = Things or Animals	Where = Place

Sentence	Who? What? Where? Question	Answer
Paul went to Alabama.	_____ went to Alabama?	Paul
Jack went to Rome.	_____ did Jack go?	To Rome
Lee had fun.	_____ did Lee do?	Have fun
Cody flew to Spain.	_____ flew to Spain?	_____
Tracy flew to Spain.	_____ went to Spain?	_____
Steve wrote home.	_____ did Steve do?	_____
Mindy ate a pear.	_____ did Mindy eat?	_____
Ty ate a banana.	_____?	_____
John took out the trash.	_____ did John do?	_____
Bob went home.	_____ did Bob go?	_____
Kate threw a ball.	_____ did Kate do?	_____
Sam went to school.	_____ went to school?	_____
Sue went to the zoo.	_____ did Sue go?	_____
Kate ate a snack.	_____ did Kate do?	_____
Jerry rode a horse.	_____ rode a horse?	_____
The dog went to the vet.	_____ did the dog go?	_____
The dog ate a bone.	_____ did the dog do?	_____
Rex the dog fell asleep.	_____ fell asleep?	_____

Read the sentence then fill in the blanks with "who, what, or where."
Don't forget your end punctuation and to capitalize names.

1. Todd ate a pear. Ally went to the store. Mary had fun.

    Example

    <u>Who</u> ate a pear?   <u>Todd</u>
    _____ went to the store?   <u>Ally</u>
    _____ did Todd eat?   <u>A pear</u>
    _____ had fun?   _____
    _____ did Mary do?   _____
    _____ did Ally go?   _____
    _____ did Todd do?   _____
    _____ did Ally do?   _____
    _____ did Mary do?   _____

2. Mike played baseball. Sue went to the zoo. John had a party.

    _____ played baseball?   _____
    _____ went to the zoo?   _____
    _____ did Mike play?   _____
    _____ had a party?   _____
    _____ did Sue go?   _____
    _____ did John have?   _____
    _____ did Mike do?   _____
    _____ did Sue do?   _____
    _____ did John do?   _____

PART EIGHT
WHO? WHAT? AND HOW?

We have already learned about "who" and "what." **HOW** refers to *the way in which something is done*. Is it done carefu**ly**, happi**ly**, or easi**ly**? Notice that the letters "**ly**" are at the end of each of these words. These are called *adverbs*.

Let's practice making some adverbs, so that we can answer the question, "how?"

Example

careful	+	ly	=	carefully
slow	+	ly	=	_____
bashful	+	ly	=	_____
sad	+	ly	=	_____
joyful	+	ly	=	_____

Answer "who, what, or how" by filling in the blanks.
Who? What? How?

Jack listened carefully.	_____ did Jack listen?	carefully
Mike listened poorly.	_____ did Mike listen?	poorly
Joe did not listen.	_____ did not listen?	Joe
Sarah whispered quietly.	_____ did Sarah whisper?	_____
Jay jumped up.	_____ did Jay do?	_____
Cindy sat down.	_____ sat down?	_____
The dog barked.	_____ barked?	_____

Who? **What?** **How?**

Jack spoke quietly.	[How?] did Jack speak?	_____
Tom sang songs.	_____ did Tom sing?	Songs
Sam did not care.	[Who?] did not care?	_____
Lisa hummed quietly.	_____ did Lisa hum?	_____
Pat sat up.	[What?] did Pat do?	_____
The cat sat down.	_____ sat down?	_____
The phone rang.	_____ rang?	The phone
Sue walked slowly.	[How?] did Sue walk?	_____
Tom ate apples.	_____ did Tom eat?	Apples
Lisa did not smile.	[Who?] did not smile?	_____
Lou loved Sarah.	_____ did Lou love?	_____
Anne did not call.	[Who?] did not call?	_____
Lisa spoke rapidly.	_____ did Lisa speak?	_____
The tree fell down.	[What?] did the tree do?	_____
The cat slept.	_____ slept?	_____
The children played.	_____ played?	_____
The bell rang.	_____ rang?	The bell

PART NINE

WHO, WHAT, WHERE, AND WHY — STORIES

Read the story and answer the questions by filling in the blanks.

> Tom broke Amy's toy, so Amy got angry. Amy told her mother, and Amy's mother sent Tom home.

Who?

Who broke Amy's toy? _____

Who got angry and told her mother? _____

Who sent Tom home? _____

What?

What did Tom break? _____

What did Amy's mother do? _____

_____

Why?

Why did Amy's mother send Tom home? _____

_____

> The kids went to the circus and ate popcorn. They met a funny clown who had three balls. The clown juggled the balls and made the kids laugh.

Who?

Who went to the circus? _____

Who ate popcorn? _____

Who had three balls? _____

Who juggled the balls? _____

Who made the kids laugh? _____

What?

What did the kids eat? _____

What did the clown have? _____

What did the clown do? _____

_____

Where?

Where did the kids go? _____

Why?

Why did the kids laugh? _____

_____

> The dogs barked at the kitten, so the kitten hid behind Susie. Susie picked up the kitten and made the dogs be quiet.

Who?

Who picked up the kitten? _____

Who made the dogs be quiet? _____

What?

What did the dogs bark at? _____

What scared the kitten? _____

What hid behind Susie? _____

What did the dogs do? _____

What did the kitten do? _____

What did Susie do? _____

_____

Why?

Why did the kitten hide behind Susie? _____

_____

> Joey's mother took him to a movie. It was a funny movie about a mouse named Tim. Joey liked the movie, and he laughed a lot.

Who?

Who took Joey to a movie? _____

Who liked the movie? _____

Who was the movie about? _____

Who laughed a lot? _____

What?

What did Joey and his mother see? _____

What was the movie about? _____

What did Joey do? _____

Where?

Where did Joey's mom take him? _____

Why?

Why did Joey laugh? _____

_____

Bob and Sue got new bicycles. They went for a ride by the river. Bob and Sue had a lot of fun riding their new bicycles.

Who?

Who got new bicycles? _____

Who went for a ride by the river? _____

Who had fun? _____

What?

What did Bob get? _____

What did Sue get? _____

What did Bob and Sue do? _____

_____

Where?

Where did Bob and Sue go? _____

_____

Why?

Why did Bob & Sue have fun? _____

_____

Mike's dad took him to the ballpark. He watched his favorite team, the Panthers, play baseball. Mike enjoyed the baseball game, and he got to eat a hot dog.

Who?

Who took Mike to the baseball park? _____

Who enjoyed the game? _____

Who watched his favorite team? _____

Who got to eat a hot dog? _____

What?

What did Mike and his dad do? _____

What was the name of Mike's favorite team? _____

What did Mike eat? _____

What did Mike watch? _____

What game did the Panthers play? _____

Why?

Why did Mike enjoy the game? _____

_____

PART TEN
WHO? WHEN? AND WHY?

Read the sentences and answer the questions. Don't forget to use correct punctuation and capitals.

Who   When   Why

The boy ran to the store early in the morning to get some eggs.

Who ran to the store? _____

When did the boy run to the store? _____

Why did the boy run to the store? _____

When the stranger approached, Rex the dog growled to scare the stranger away.

Who growled? _____

When did the dog growl? _____

Why did the dog growl at the stranger? _____

_____

Who   When   Why

The baby cried to get attention when he was hungry.

Who cried?
_____

When did the baby cry?
_____

Why did the baby cry?
_____

The man ran fast when he saw the mailman because he wanted to get his mail.

Who ran fast?
_____

When did the man run?
_____

Why did the man run fast?
_____

Who   When   Why

Max the dog wagged his tail when he wanted his owner to pet him.

Who wagged his tail?
_____

When did the dog wag his tail?
_____

Why did the dog wag his tail?
_____

The girl ate an ice cream cone at lunch because it was hot outside.

Who ate an ice cream cone?
_____

When did the girl eat an ice cream cone?
_____

Why did the girl eat an ice cream cone?
_____

Who   When   Why

The little boy got a brand new truck on Christmas day because he was good all year.

Who got a brand new truck?
_____

When did the little boy get a brand new truck?
_____

Why did the little boy get a new truck?
_____

Grandmother got a special cake on her birthday because she was one-hundred years old.

Who got a special cake?
_____

When did grandmother get a special cake?
_____

Why did grandmother get a special cake on her birthday?
_____

PART ELEVEN
REASONING WHY

As we learned, when we read something with the word "because" in it, it's easy to tell *why* something happened. For example, the dog bit the girl because she pulled his tail. Why did the dog bite the girl? *Because* she pulled his tail.

However, we can still reason *why* something happened even when we don't see the word "because." This is sometimes called *"cause* and *effect."* What this means is when one thing happens, another thing happens next. Once we know the *cause* and *effect*, we can guess *why* something happened.

For example, when the girl pulled the dogs tail, the dog bit her. First, the girl pulled the dogs tail. Next, the dog bit her. Therefore, we can *reason* that the dog bit the girl *because* he did not like having his tail pulled. Why did the dog bite the girl? Because she pulled his tail!

Let's practice identifying cause and effect.

Example

The boy skinned his knee, and it hurt. The boy started to cry.

What happened first? (Cause)	<u>The boy skinned his knee</u>.
What happened next? (Effect)	<u>It hurt.</u>

Why do boys cry when they skin their knees?
<u>Because it hurts.</u>

Joey told a lie, and his mom got angry.

What happened first? (Cause)   Joey told a lie.

What happened next? (Effect)   _____

Why is it bad to tell lies?
Because it makes people angry.

Susan forgot to wear her safety helmet when she rode her bicycle. She fell off and hurt her head.

What happened first? (Cause)   Susan forgot to wear her safety helmet.

What happened next? (Effect)   _____

Why is it important to wear a safety helmet?
So you don't hurt your head.

Lee spilled his drink on the floor, and it made a mess.

What happened first? (Cause)   _____
What happened next? (Effect)   _____

Why don't we want to spill our drinks?
Because it makes a mess.

Jay played with a knife, and he cut his hand.

    What happened first? (Cause) _____

    What happened next? (Effect) _____

    Why is it bad to play with knives?
    Because you might cut your hand.

The sun came out in the morning, and it melted the snow.

    What happened first? (Cause) _____

    What happened next? (Effect) _____

    Why did the snow melt?
    Because _____

Amy put on her pretty new dress. She looked in the mirror and smiled.

    What happened first? (Cause) _____

    What happened next? (Effect) _____

    Why was Amy happy?
    Because she was wearing a pretty new dress.

Read the sentences and try to reason why.

When Joey told a lie, his mom got mad.

Why is it bad to tell lies?

_____

When kids don't wear safety helmets, they sometimes get hurt.

Why is it important to wear a safety helmet?

_____

It is cold when it snows, so you should wear a coat to stay warm.

Why do we wear coats when it snows?

_____

When it rains, we use umbrellas to stay dry.

Why do we use umbrellas in the rain?

_____

When we have trouble seeing things, we wear glasses.

Why do people wear glasses?

_____

When Tom found a penny, he started to laugh.

Why did Tom laugh?

_____

When other kids are very noisy, it's hard to get your work done.

Why is it important for kids to be quiet?

_____

It is hot in the summer, so you should wear shorts.

Why do we wear shorts in the summer?

_____

When we get hungry, we eat a snack.

Why do we eat snacks?

_____

When we get lost, we ask for directions.

Why do people ask for directions?

_____

PART TWELVE
PUTTING IT ALL TOGETHER

WHAT　　　WHEN　　　WHY　　　WHERE

Look at the pictures and answer the "wh" questions.

Why is the duck wet?
_____
_____

Where is the toothpaste?
_____
_____

Who is holding a book?
_____
_____

What is this man doing?
_____
_____

Who is standing on a surf board? _____

Where is the surf board? _____

What is the boy playing with? _____

Why is he smiling? _____

The squirrel's name is Bob.

Where are the squirrel's glasses? _____

What is the squirrel doing? _____

What color are the squirrel's glasses? _____

What color is the book? _____

Who is reading a book? _____

Why is the squirrel wearing glasses? _____
_____

When does the squirrel wear his glasses? _____
_____

When do we see Santa Claus? (What holiday?)
_____

54

Where are these kids playing?

   a. at the zoo

   b. on a snowy hill

   c. in the kitchen

What are they making?
_____

Why are they wearing coats, hats, and gloves?
_____

Who is fixing the snowman's eye?

   a. a girl in a red hat

   b. a baby in a stroller

   c. the snowman is fixing his own eye.

What do you see behind the snowman?

   a. a penguin

   b. three kids on a sled

   c. all of the above

When do we build snowmen?

   a. in the summer

   b. in the winter

Where do we go to see a teacher?

   a. to the circus

   b. to school

   c. to the grocery store

What is this teacher holding?
_____

Why are her glasses crooked?
_____

Who is writing on the chalkboard?

   a. the kids

   b. the principal

   c. the teacher

What do you see on the chalkboard?

   a. letters

   b. clouds

   c. numbers

When do children go to school?

   a. during the day

   b. at night

   c. after dinner

Where are these children sitting?

   a. at a table

   b. by a campfire

   c. on the beach

What are the kids getting ready to do?
_____

Why is the little girl cutting the cake?
_____

Who is standing and holding a green plate?

   a. the little boy in the red, striped shirt

   b. the mother in a blue dress

   c. the little girl in a yellow dress

What do you see on the table?

   a. toys

   b. macaroni and cheese

   c. plates, napkins, and cake

When do we eat birthday cake?

   a. at Christmas

   b. on someone's birthday

   c. at Easter

Where is this girl?

   a. on a bed

   b. at a desk

   c. next to a tree

What color is the girl's dress?

_____

Why is the little girl holding a pencil?

_____

Who is writing on a piece of paper?

   a. the teacher

   b. no one

   c. the girl

What else do you see on the desk?

   a. a stack of books

   b. an eraser

   c. a computer

When will the girl put the pencil down?

   a. when she is done writing

   b. when the pencil falls down

Where are these kids?

  a. in the mountains

  b. at the zoo

  c. at the beach

What is the little girl sitting on?

_____

Why is the little girl wearing a bathing suit?

_____

What is the little girl rubbing on her arm?

  a. ketchup

  b. sunscreen

  c. shampoo

What do you see above their heads?

  a. water

  b. grass

  c. a blue umbrella

When do we play at the beach?

  a. when it is warm outside

  b. when it is cold outside

Where is this girl standing?

    a. on a trampoline

    b. beside a castle

    c. in front of a lake

What is she looking at?

_____

Why is her hair dry?

_____

Who is taking the picture?

    a. a pair of ducks

    b. another person

    c. a tree

    d. no one

What do you see in the background?

    a. green trees

    b. rolling hills

    c. calm water

    d. all of the above

When was the picture taken?

    a. on a nice, sunny day

    b. on a cold, rainy day

> Answer these "WH" questions about yourself.

Be sure to write complete sentences.

What is your first name?

<u>**My first name is**</u> _____

What is your last name?

_____

Where do you go to school?

_____

What is your favorite movie?

_____

Why is it your favorite movie?

_____

What is your favorite book?

_____

Why is it your favorite book?

_____

What is your favorite color?

_____

What are you wearing today?

_____

When do you go to bed?

_____

When do you brush your teeth?

_____

When do you eat lunch?

_____

When do you eat breakfast?

_____

Where do you live?

_____

Who is your mom?

_____

Who is your dad?

_____

Who is your best friend?

_____

When is your birthday?

_____

What is your favorite holiday?

_____

What is your favorite toy?

_____

Suggested Follow Up Activities

Activity One

Go on a walk with your teacher. Your teacher will point to things and ask you "wh" questions. Try to answer all of the questions.

Activity Two

Get out a bunch of toys with your teacher or a friend. Take turns holding up each toy and asking and answering "wh" questions. For example, "What is this toy?" "Who does this toy belong to?" "Where does this toy go?" "When would you play with this toy?"

Activity Three

Find a picture book. Look at the pictures and write down as many "wh" questions and answers as you can.

Activity Four

Write all the "wh" question words on a stack of note cards and sit across the table from a friend. Take turns asking and answering "wh" questions. For example, "What is your name?" "Where do you go to school?"

(Hint: You may need an additional set of note cards with subject cues on them such as friends, family, games, and school. For example, if you are given the "WHO" wh-card and "FAMILY" subject-card, your question might be, "Who is your dad?")

Data Collection & Notes

Date _____   Lesson # **Part One** _____
                                Page(s) _____

% of accuracy _____   Suggestions: Repeat Lesson
# of prompts _____   Review Lesson
                                              Other _____

Observations
_____
_____
_____
_____

Other
_____
_____
_____
_____

Name or Initials of teacher/tutor _____

- -

Date _____   Lesson # **Part Two** _____
                                Page(s) _____

% of accuracy _____   Suggestions: Repeat Lesson
# of prompts _____   Review Lesson
                                              Other _____

Observations
_____
_____
_____
_____

Other
_____
_____
_____
_____

Name or Initials of teacher/tutor _____

Date _____ Lesson # __Part Three__
                             Page(s) _____

% of accuracy _____ Suggestions: Repeat Lesson
# of prompts _____   Review Lesson
                                           Other _____

Observations
_____
_____
_____
_____

Other
_____
_____
_____
_____

Name or Initials of teacher/tutor _____

- -

Date _____ Lesson # __Part Four__
                             Page(s) _____

% of accuracy _____ Suggestions: Repeat Lesson
# of prompts _____   Review Lesson
                                           Other _____

Observations
_____
_____
_____
_____

Other
_____
_____
_____
_____

Name or Initials of teacher/tutor _____

Date _____ Lesson # __Part Five__
                             Page(s) _____

% of accuracy _____ Suggestions: Repeat Lesson
# of prompts _____   Review Lesson
                                       Other _____

Observations
_____
_____
_____
_____

Other
_____
_____
_____
_____

Name or Initials of teacher/tutor _____

- -

Date _____ Lesson # __Part Six__
                             Page(s) _____

% of accuracy _____ Suggestions: Repeat Lesson
# of prompts _____   Review Lesson
                                       Other _____

Observations
_____
_____
_____
_____

Other
_____
_____
_____
_____

Name or Initials of teacher/tutor _____

Date _____ Lesson # __Part Seven__
                             Page(s) _____

% of accuracy _____ Suggestions: Repeat Lesson
# of prompts _____   Review Lesson
                                           Other _____

Observations

_____
_____
_____
_____

Other

_____
_____
_____
_____

Name or Initials of teacher/tutor _____

- -

Date _____ Lesson # __Part Eight__
                             Page(s) _____

% of accuracy _____ Suggestions: Repeat Lesson
# of prompts _____   Review Lesson
                                           Other _____

Observations

_____
_____
_____
_____

Other

_____
_____
_____
_____

Name or Initials of teacher/tutor _____

Date _____ Lesson # **Part Nine** _____
                                                          Page(s) _____

% of accuracy _____   Suggestions: Repeat Lesson
# of prompts _____   Review Lesson
                                                                Other _____

Observations

_____
_____
_____
_____

Other

_____
_____
_____
_____

Name or Initials of teacher/tutor _____

Date _____ Lesson # **Part Ten** _____
                                                          Page(s) _____

% of accuracy _____   Suggestions: Repeat Lesson
# of prompts _____   Review Lesson
                                                                Other _____

Observations

_____
_____
_____
_____

Other

_____
_____
_____
_____

Name or Initials of teacher/tutor _____

Date _____   Lesson # __Part Eleven__
                              Page(s) _____

% of accuracy _____   Suggestions: Repeat Lesson
# of prompts _____   Review Lesson
                                            Other _____

Observations
_____
_____
_____
_____

Other
_____
_____
_____
_____

Name or Initials of teacher/tutor _____

- -

Date _____   Lesson # __Part Twelve__
                              Page(s) _____

% of accuracy _____   Suggestions: Repeat Lesson
# of prompts _____   Review Lesson
                                            Other _____

Observations
_____
_____
_____
_____

Other
_____
_____
_____
_____

Name or Initials of teacher/tutor _____

Date _____   Lesson # __Activity One__
                                   Page(s) _____

% of accuracy _____   Suggestions: Repeat Lesson
# of prompts _____   Review Lesson
                                                 Other _____

Observations
_____
_____
_____
_____

Other
_____
_____
_____
_____

Name or Initials of teacher/tutor _____

- -

Date _____   Lesson # __Activity Two__
                                   Page(s) _____

% of accuracy _____   Suggestions: Repeat Lesson
# of prompts _____   Review Lesson
                                                 Other _____

Observations
_____
_____
_____
_____

Other
_____
_____
_____
_____

Name or Initials of teacher/tutor _____

Date _____ Lesson # __Activity Three__
                             Page(s) _____

% of accuracy _____ Suggestions: Repeat Lesson
# of prompts _____   Review Lesson
                                          Other _____

Observations

_____
_____
_____
_____

Other

_____
_____
_____
_____

Name or Initials of teacher/tutor _____

- -

Date _____ Lesson # __Activity Four__
                             Page(s) _____

% of accuracy _____ Suggestions: Repeat Lesson
# of prompts _____   Review Lesson
                                          Other _____

Observations

_____
_____
_____
_____

Other

_____
_____
_____
_____

Name or Initials of teacher/tutor _____

Date _____   Lesson # _____
                                Page(s) _____

% of accuracy _____   Suggestions: Repeat Lesson
# of prompts _____   Review Lesson
                                               Other _____

Observations

_____
_____
_____
_____

Other

_____
_____
_____
_____

Name or Initials of teacher/tutor _____

- -

Date _____   Lesson # _____
                                Page(s) _____

% of accuracy _____   Suggestions: Repeat Lesson
# of prompts _____   Review Lesson
                                               Other _____

Observations

_____
_____
_____
_____

Other

_____
_____
_____
_____

Name or Initials of teacher/tutor _____

OTHER AVAILABLE WORKBOOKS AND MATERIALS

The *Nashoba's Learning System* includes a series of Language Expansion, Math Curriculum, and Reading Comprehension Workbooks designed to provide educators and parents with readily available tools to help teach children on the Autism Spectrum or children with visual, concrete learning styles.

The hands-on series was designed to be used without the need for further lesson planning or a formal teaching background and to travel easily with the child between learning environments.

For further information and to see new releases, please visit:
http://www.nashobasworkbooks.com